My First Pet Library from the **American Humane Association**

My First Fish

American Humane®

*Protecting
Children & Animals
Since 1877*

Enslow Elementary
an imprint of
Enslow Publishers, Inc.
40 Industrial Road
Box 398
Berkeley Heights, NJ 07922
USA

http://www.enslow.com

Linda Bozzo

American Humane.

**Protecting
Children & Animals
Since 1877**

Founded in 1877, the American Humane Association is the oldest national organization dedicated to protecting both children and animals. Through a network of child and animal protection agencies and individuals, the American Humane Association develops policies, legislation, curricula, and training programs to protect children and animals from abuse, neglect, and exploitation. To learn how you can support the vision of a nation where no child or animal will ever be a victim of willful abuse or neglect, visit www.americanhumane.org, phone (303) 792-9900, or write to the American Humane Association at 63 Inverness Drive East, Englewood, Colorado, 80112-5117.

● ●

This book is dedicated to my husband and daughters who never stop believing in me, and to pet lovers everywhere.

● ●

Library of Congress Cataloging-in-Publication Data

Bozzo, Linda.
   My first fish / Linda Bozzo.
      p. cm. — (My first pet library from the American Humane Association)
   Includes bibliographical references and index.
   ISBN-13: 978-0-7660-2751-0
   ISBN-10: 0-7660-2751-1
      1. Aquarium fishes—Juvenile literature.
   I. Title. II. Series: Bozzo, Linda. My first pet library from the American Humane Association.
   SF457.25B69 2007
   639.34—dc22   2006010500

Printed in the United States of America

10 9 8 7 6 5 4 3 2 1

To Our Readers: We have done our best to make sure all Internet Addresses in this book were active and appropriate when we went to press. However, the author and the publisher have no control over and assume no liability for the material available on those Internet sites or on other Web sites they may link to. Any comments or suggestions can be sent by e-mail to comments@enslow.com or to the address on the back cover.

Every effort has been made to locate all copyright holders of material used in this book. If any errors or omissions have occurred, corrections will be made in future editions of this book.

Illustration Credits: 1996–2005 Art Today, Inc., p. 12; Myrleen Ferguson Cate/PhotoEdit, p. 15; Nicole diMella/Enslow Publishers, Inc., p. 14 (top); © 2006 Jupiterimages, p. 24; Michael Newman/PhotoEdit, pp. 8, 20 (top); Shutterstock, pp. 1, 3, 5, 7, 9, 11, 13 (bottom), 14 (bottom), 16, 17, 18, 19, 20 (bottom), 21, 23, 25, 26, 27, 28, 31.

Cover Credits: Shutterstock.

Contents

Fish Can Be Fun

Looking at a tank full of colorful fish can be fun. Fish, like all pets, need care. If you do not have a lot of time to spend with a pet, a fish may be a good pet for you.

Before you dive in, take time to learn all about your new pet. This book can help answer questions you may have about finding and caring for your new pet fish.

Fish swim in a clean tank.

What Kind of Fish Do I Want?

Fish come in many shapes, sizes, and colors. Some fish like to be with other fish. These fish live in a **community tank**. Some fish need to be kept alone.

Goldfish can live in unheated water. Most **tropical** fish need warm water. They also need more care. Marine fish will need to live in saltwater.

Some fish need water treated with special chemicals. This makes the water safe for the fish.

These pale yellow fish swim with each other in their community tank.

Make sure the fish you get at the pet store look healthy before taking them home.

You can buy fish from a pet store. The tanks in the store should be clean. The fish should look healthy. A sick fish may swim on its side or upside down. It may have sores on its fins or body.

Some fish swim near the bottom of the tank.

What Will My New Fish Need?

Some fish, like Bettas, can be kept in a fish bowl. Most fish need a **tank** with lots of room to swim. Ask a person at the pet store which is best for your fish.

A light for your tank will help you see your fish better. If you put special plants in your tank, a light can also help these plants to grow. A cover for your tank will keep your fish from jumping out. It will also keep dust and other pets from getting in.

Community tanks can be very colorful.

A **filter** and an **air pump** will keep the water clean. Some fish need to live in warm water. If this is the kind of fish you pick, you will need a heater. A special **thermometer** tells you if the water temperature is right for your fish.

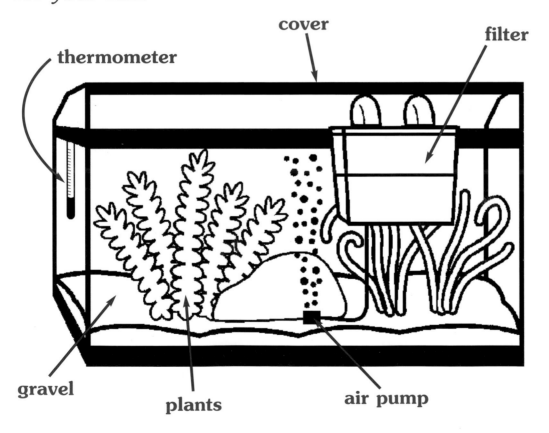

You may need these parts for your fish tank.

Your fish will need help getting used to the temperature of their new home. Float the bag, with your new fish in it, in the tank for five to ten minutes. Open the bag to add some water from the tank. Close it again and wait five more minutes.

Now you use a net to gently take your fish out of the bag. Then put them into the tank. Do not add the water from the bag to the tank.

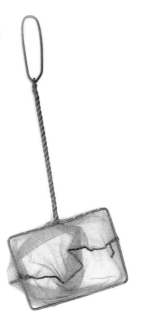

You can also buy **gravel** and plants for your tank. Safe decorations will make your tank fun for your fish.

Different fish eat different foods. Ask a person at the pet store what food is best for your fish.

This is one kind of fish food. Ask someone at a pet store what is best for your fish.

gravel

You can learn a
lot about your
fish by watching
it every day.

How Often Should I Feed My Fish?

It is best to feed your fish once or twice a day. Drop a small amount of food in the tank. If your fish eat all the food in two to three minutes, they may need more food. Be careful not to feed your fish too much. This can hurt your fish.

Red and silver fish swim in a clean tank.

Goldfish like to swim in tanks.

Where Should I Keep My New Pet?

Your pet's new home should be set up a few days before you bring your fish home. After you have filled the tank with treated tap water, ask a person at the pet store to test it to be sure it is safe for your fish.

This fish must be in a bowl by itself. It is a Siamese fighting fish, or Betta. It will fight with other fish.

Place your fish tank where everyone can see it.

Red cap oranada goldfish

These are two different kinds of goldfish.

The tank should not be placed in sunlight. It should be kept away from heating and cooling vents. Set the tank near an electrical outlet. It will need a strong table or stand to rest on. Once you fill the tank with water, it will be too heavy to move.

How Can I Keep My New Fish Healthy?

Take time to check your pet every day. See that everything is working. Check the water temperature. Just like you, fish can get sick. Each day, see that your fish look healthy. If you think your fish may be sick, talk to a **vet** or a person at the pet store.

Do not tap on the tank or bowl. This can scare and hurt the fish.

Neon tetra fish swim by the community tank plants.

Ask an adult to help you clean the tank.

Each week, the inside walls of the tank should be cleaned. You can use a special tool called an **algae** scraper. Scrape the inside walls of the tank.

Once a month, the gravel should be cleaned. Add water treated with special chemicals at the right temperature.

Clean tank walls
help keep your
fish healthy.

Take Care of Your Fish

Having fish to look after can be lots of fun. You and your friends can spend hours watching your fish swim and dive. Take care of your fish. They can add color to your home and can be fun for your family.

Fish need love and care just like you do.
This is a lion head goldfish.

Lion fish

Words to Know

air pump—A pump that blows air through the water in the fish tank.

algae—A plantlike living thing that can grow on fish tank walls.

community tank—A tank where different kinds of fish live together.

filter—Keeps the water in the fish tank clear and fresh.

gravel—Small pieces of rock placed at the bottom of the tank. Gravel also helps filter and hold dirt and dust.

tank—A container with clear sides for fish to live.

thermometer—An instrument used to measure the temperature of the water in a tank.

tropical—A warm environment. Tropical fish need warm water.

vet—Vet is short for veterinarian, a doctor who takes care of animals.

Read About

BOOKS

Blackaby, Susan. *Fish for You: Caring For Your Fish*. Minneapolis, Minn: Picture Window Books, 2003.

Frost, Helen. *Fish*. Mankato, Minn: Pebble Books, 2001.

Loves, June. *Fish*. Philadelphia, Pa.: Chelsea Clubhouse, 2004.

Lundblad, Kristina, and Bobbie Kalman. *Animals Called Fish*. New York: Crabtree Pub. Co., 2005.

Macken, JoAnn Early. *Goldfish*. Milwaukee, Wis.: Weekly Reader Early Learning Library, 2004.

Nelson, Robin. *Pet Fish*. Minneapolis, Minn.: Lerner Publications Co., 2003.

INTERNET ADDRESSES

American Humane Association
   <http://www.americanhumane.org>
   Read about how you can help animals.

ASPCA: Animaland
   <http://www.animaland.org>
   Learn more about pet care at this site.

Index